D0846040

ANIMAL SAFARI

Cranes

by Megan Borgert-Spaniol

BLASTOFF! READERS

Note to Librarians, Teachers, and Parents:

Blastoff! Readers are carefully developed by literacy experts and combine standards-based content with developmentally appropriate text.

Level 1 provides the most support through repetition of high-frequency words, light text, predictable sentence patterns, and strong visual support.

Level 2 offers early readers a bit more challenge through varied simple sentences, increased text load, and less repetition of high-frequency words.

Level 3 advances early-fluent readers toward fluency through increased text and concept load, less reliance on visuals, longer sentences, and more literary language.

Level 4 builds reading stamina by providing more text per page, increased use of punctuation, greater variation in sentence patterns, and increasingly challenging vocabulary.

Level 5 encourages children to move from "learning to read" to "reading to learn" by providing even more text, varied writing styles, and less familiar topics.

Whichever book is right for your reader, Blastoff! Readers are the perfect books to build confidence and encourage a love of reading that will last a lifetime!

This edition first published in 2016 by Bellwether Media, Inc.

No part of this publication may be reproduced in whole or in part without written permission of the publisher. For information regarding permission, write to Bellwether Media, Inc., Attention: Permissions Department, 5357 Penn Avenue South, Minneapolis, MN 55419.

Library of Congress Cataloging-in-Publication Data

Borgert-Spaniol, Megan, 1989- author.
  Cranes / by Megan Borgert-Spaniol.
    pages cm. – (Blastoff! Readers. Animal Safari)
  Summary: "Developed by literacy experts for students in kindergarten through grade three, this book introduces cranes to young readers through leveled text and related photos"– Provided by publisher.
  Audience: Ages 5-8
  Audience: K to grade 3
  Includes bibliographical references and index.
  ISBN 978-1-62617-211-1 (hardcover: alk. paper)
  1. Cranes (Birds)–Juvenile literature. I. Title. II. Series: Blastoff! readers. 1, Animal safari.
  QL696.G84B67 2016
  598.3'2–dc23
                                                              2015004206

Text copyright © 2016 by Bellwether Media, Inc. BLASTOFF! READERS and associated logos are trademarks and/or registered trademarks of Bellwether Media, Inc. SCHOLASTIC, CHILDREN'S PRESS, and associated logos are trademarks and/or registered trademarks of Scholastic Inc.

Printed in the United States of America, North Mankato, MN.

Contents

What Are Cranes?

Cranes are tall birds. They have long legs and necks.

They live in fields, wetlands, and grasslands.

Food

Cranes eat plants and **insects** on land. They find fish and **shellfish** in water.

A crane pokes **prey** with its **bill**. It also uses the bill to dig for food.

Flocks

Cranes travel in **flocks**. They use different calls to talk.

13

Some flocks fly to warmer places for winter. They travel thousands of miles.

Crane Dance

Male and female cranes dance together. They bow, leap, and flap their wings.

Chicks

Females build nests
for their eggs.
Chicks **hatch**
a month later.

eggs

Foxes, eagles, and other **predators** hunt chicks. Parents use sharp **claws** to protect their babies. Ouch!

Glossary

bill—the hard outer part of the mouth of a bird

claws—sharp, curved nails at the end of an animal's fingers and toes

flocks—groups of cranes that travel together

hatch—to break out of an egg

insects—small animals with six legs and hard outer bodies; insect bodies are divided into three parts.

predators—animals that hunt other animals for food

prey—animals that are hunted by other animals for food

shellfish—animals that live in water and have shells; shrimp, clams, and crabs are types of shellfish.

To Learn More

AT THE LIBRARY

Borgert-Spaniol, Megan. *Flamingos.*
Minneapolis, Minn.: Bellwether Media, 2014.

George, Jean Craighead. *Luck.* New York,
N.Y.: Laura Geringer Books, 2006.

Yeoman, John. *The Heron and the Crane.*
London, U.K.: Andersen Press, 2011.

ON THE WEB

Learning more about
cranes is as easy as 1, 2, 3.

1. Go to www.factsurfer.com.

2. Enter "cranes" into the search box.

3. Click the "Surf" button and you will see a
   list of related web sites.

With factsurfer.com, finding more information
is just a click away.

Index

The images in this book are reproduced through the courtesy of: Kamonrat, front cover, p. 5; R. Gino Santa Maria, p. 7 (top); Lynne Nicholson, p. 7 (bottom left); Zack Frank, p. 7 (bottom center); biletskiy, p. 7 (bottom right); Tom & Pat Leeson/ Age Fotostock, p. 9; Maggy Meyer, p. 9 (bottom left); iliuta goean, p. 9 (bottom center); Anton Watman, p. 9 (bottom right); chuvipro, p. 11; Top Photo Group/ Age Fotostock, p. 13; qingqing, p. 15; manjeet & yograj jadeja/ Alamy, p. 17; David W. Leindecker, p. 19 (top); npine, p. 19 (bottom); Kimimasa Mayama/ Corbis, p. 21 (top); Andrey Starostin, p. 21 (bottom); Ian Rentoul, p. 21 (bottom left); jurra8, p. 21 (bottom center); Sandy Hedgepath, p. 21 (bottom right).